conclusions
delusions
and
musings on time

Poems
Christian Scott Green

ISBN: 978-0-578-89859-9

for my mother, who believed in this book

for my grandmother, who is no longer
here to read it

Contents

"Mankind is like verses written
Upon the surface of the rills."

- Gibran

"For each ecstatic instant
We must an anguish pay
In keen and quivering ratio
To the ecstasy."

- Dickinson

"... So we are grasped by what we cannot grasp."

- Rilke

Rise (with Claudia)

A fan whirs.
It HUMS......
Chanting electric mantra.
A futile distraction in the face of an unfathomable silence.
Its tireless blades carve the still air at dizzying speed,
spitting man-made wind, as if anything is possible.

And just outside the window, the natural world awakens.
Chattering and chirping, commencing her daily work.

A lamp glows.
Uncontested and alone. Refusing the dark.
Its synthetic light, once a beacon, will soon be humbled,
eclipsed by a burning star, ninety million miles away.

And just outside the window, the patient morning stretches.
Expanding imperceptibly, warming the earth.

A clock ticks.
Relentless. Soulless.
Its toothed wheels in a mechanical dance, spinning time.
Its hands, scoring straight lines on the formless everything,
trying desperately to measure the infinite.

And just outside the window, the people rise again,
to play as gods, dream up meaning, and flee certain death
in an unknown forever.

From Chaos

I fled the grid, in need of more time to think,
on my quest for perfection and order,
to this primeval place, where man's but a guest,
seeking answers in silence and still.

But chittering robins have roused me from reverie,
bobbing for treasures in dirt;
they hop in quick bursts over clusters of clover
indiscriminately drawn on the grass.

A flurry of bugs spins synchronous circles,
illuminated flecks in the sun.
Rorschach clouds blot a pale blue canvas,
enigmas in tranquil disorder.

Ants gone rogue, who've abandoned their posts,
march unfettered to invisible drums,
yet navigate deftly the burgeoning weeds
climbing out of small clefts in the stone.

Fearless squirrels trace inchoate spirals
as they play and give chase through the trees
that stand shoulder to shoulder, rooted together,
arms joined in felicitous embrace.

A haphazard thicket of tall purple flowers
sways passionately, a choir in song.
Singing the praises of a world which fulfills
every detail, if left to itself.

As gas lamps ignite, marking time with a hiss,
my mind stirs and cognition resumes.
From a whisper amidst this evocative chaos
an epiphany, initiated, blooms.

Pursuit and Recollection

Waking life passes
Eyes fastened forward
Pursuance consumes.

Energy exhausted
Wading through the *was*
Recollections exhumed.

Blind to the actual
Numb to the tactile
Beatitude eludes.

I, Love

I am grand. I am blind.
I break hearts, and I mend.
I'm the source, destination,
Beginning, and end.

I am simply complex,
I'm in flux, I'm inert.
I am given to taking,
I give 'til it hurts.

I am torment and joy,
I'm a scream, an embrace.
I am savage and wicked,
A moment of grace.

I am carefully held,
I am carelessly lost.
I'm surrender complete,
I'm revenge at all cost.

I am worth every minute,
I'm the slayer of time.
I'm a passion soon buried,
I am routine sublimed.

I'm connection, reflection,
Two sides of one thing.
I'm the dark night of winter,
The light breath of spring.

I am work, never finished.
I'm the journey back home.
I am never indifferent,
I am never alone.

I am Love.

Combustible

in their tiny box
two hearts
do a careful dance
moving around the issues
keeping the necessary distance
keeping a lot to themselves
too much unwanted friction
could burn the whole thing down.

Withheld

If touch has the power to heal,
surely this must be murder.

Inside of an Hour

How does one live in the space of an hour,
thrown from the brink, cascading through symbol,
a fleeting expression, evanescent grit,
sole blink of the cosmic eye?

A trace caught in glass, be it window or mirror.
where consciousness flips on and off like a switch,
while time, at play, somersaults forever:
head over feet over head...

Balloons become teardrops, gravity sets in.
What measure of life can be squeezed between voids?
Burst from the womb, on a path to return.
Birth and death joined at the gut.

Choice, an illusion! A balm to soothe madness.
The mightiest will is mere fodder at best:
cattle, paraded in file to slaughter,
blood, in vein, flowing back to the heart,
rivers, caught up in their visions of grandeur,
swallowed by the mouth of the sea.

As dust begets dust and synapses collapse,
does one grasp at meaning, for love, or for purchase?
Is the weight of a moment made less by its counting?
What matters inside of an hour?

Bathtub

A simple bug,
with simple brain,
stuck squirming on its back.

No means to
contemplate the drain,
there's some relief in that.

To Catch a Phrase

An expedition.
In search of a worthy tale,
I set sail on the bountiful sea,
pray skill and providence both serve me well -
O brilliant lighthouse, guide my way!
Pacing the deck, I gaze out past the bulwark,
cautious, on guard, against mutiny within,
and though carefully plotted, no course is assured;
I must remain steadfast, but pay heed the wind.

I lift my head up, turn my face toward the clouds.
Glorious words swim behind my eyes,
infinite variations, myriad shapes,
the foremost - allusions, or more than themselves.
Some dart and pirouette, just below the surface,
others plunge to extraordinary depths.
Many run out the line, a few hold their ground.
In well traveled waters lurk elusive bests.

Mythical serpents, old beasts of tradition,
spin ruinous maelstroms, wreak havoc with doubt;
discouraging those sailors with weak constitutions,
turning ships back to the safety of land.
But an apprehensive life? What a dreadful sentence!
To capture those phrases deserving of lore,
I shall cast out my net, prove myself captain,
set down my words, may they live evermore.

Conductor

Leaves rest on branches, notes
on the staff, untold symphonies within,
holding the keys to immemorial music
written on the backs of generations.

Orchestras in repose wait on the Wind;
She, that phantom, ethereal muse,
ineffable master of improvisation,
youthful spirit as old as sound.

Will she build to crescendo, or storm in at once?
Gentle or malevolent, she stirs the world.
With each breath taken, she speaks revelation.
The trees stand ready to strike up their boughs...

One Consequence of Speed

A race is on to fold the sky at will,
obliterate the distance between points.
When A is B, no path, and no resistance,
too late, we'll see there's beauty in the difference.

Future Transgressions (a rant)

...pads and pods
and
phones and drones
and
snaps and apps
and
texts and tweets
and
one more gram
as if you'll die
if you happen to miss
just one small piece
of these inconsequential
inhuman connections
as Art dies around you
in every direction
keep listening to books
and keep looking at songs
the time to build character
spent so they stare at you
this world seems happy
just clapping along...

Feast

A feast for the eyes,
a unique confection.
Each detail fulfilled,
a Kingdom's perfection.

Robust and rotund,
full feathers of black.
Iridescent, with white tips
splayed in the back.

A small head and face,
both rendered in blue.
Azure bleeds to pink
in such delicate hues.

He's there, can you see him,
his sentient gaze?
A being, alive,
not a thing, nor a taste.

Not human, like us,
who carry the seed
to murder for pleasure,
not solely for need.

Even calling it sport
does falsely imply
either side may prevail
and it's not genocide.

When necessities change
as our species evolves,
true proof of ascent
should be to dissolve

old customs of cruelty
and shameful abuse,
to cite "ugly and dumb",
a convenient excuse.

Empathy demands
a high functioning brain:
the tool that we flaunt
at the top of the chain.

When hunger's been sated
see past his demise.
Devour his beauty.
A feast, for the eyes!

Breach

Reconnaissance
intimated a breach.
Now you're hurling
accusations like bombs.
Rage twists your face
beyond recognition.
Truth hangs
in the air like smoke.
Regret fills the chasm between us.

But I seek no cover,
offer no defense.
Words will not lessen the damage.
My intent seems a meager bandage.

Impostor

Who wore a smile that never quite fit,
their heart torn to bits on this sleeve?

Who wore holes in tender souls,
walking over them in these shoes?

Who wore down these aching bones,
dancing with madness and the moon?

Who warred with sin in this thin raddled skin,
fed delusion with a silver spoon?

Who won't forgive this pained reflection -
even look him in the eye?

Who is this woeful stranger
I do not recognize?

Forfeit

We forfeit everything and call it hope.
With this hope, fill our glasses
now strangely empty.
We fill our time with the concrete.
We build up walls and still call it living.

We make new beds to lie in.
We make new art. We make new love.
We trade the ecstatic for safety and prudence,
color inside the lines.

We jump through hoops,
go through the motions.
We walk new roads one step at a time;
drink life through a straw, and label it progress,
but feel like we're dying of thirst.

Presence

Experience - What has been - What ever will be -

Every sound - Every spectacle - Each extraordinary thing -

A universe entire - In one single breath.

Bridges

We shared
first a glance,
then shared in the risk.
We traveled the path
between ritual and rapture.
We shared of our bodies,
laid bare our souls,
fought for each other,
exceeded our sum.

Now we share in the fear
of who will go first,
and if it will hurt,
and what of us lasts.

But my darling, my friend,
we loved and we mattered.
Take solace in knowing
you were never alone.

My Dearest

Come to me, I beg of thee;
hold me through the dark of night.
Lurking near, yet still I fear
thy absence and the morning light.

I give thee chase, my need goes weeks,
can't climb my way to slumber's peak.
Collapsed in an exhausted heap.
Come to me my dearest, Sleep.

Between the Devil and the Deep

six a.m.
Hell follows.
wave swallows wave,
thousands crash the shore.
ends come quickly. murder is easy.
the dead, the near dead, the empty inside,
lie half-buried, shells along the beach.

knotted stomachs smear the sand in hideous abstract.
Red and Green transmute into grotesque hues.
unformed lives take unnameable shapes.
what god could possibly allow this?
what mother could bear to look?

innocent boys disguised as men,
dressed up like means to an end.

For Virgil

Swim,
as fast and as far as you can.
In any direction.
In every direction.

Be, just
as you should.
And do not trouble your noble heart,
or fear you need return,
for I can still see you from here.

This is Now

What use are proofs to me,
rocket ships, and galaxies,
if there's no "you and I"?
As far as I can see,
your smile dwarfs the sky.

Is your laughter just a gift,
a sweet distraction from what is?
Or a glimpse of lasting magic
we inhabit in some great beyond?

I can't wrap my head around it,
I'll just wrap my arms around you.
This is now.
Who needs forever?

What good are church and shrine,
Elysian Fields, or god's design,
without you in my heart?
We may not be divine,
but you're a work of art.

Does infinity exist
within a moment, as we kiss?
Is love the apogee,
and death just buried bones?
Or planted seed?

I can't wrap my head around it,
I'll just wrap my arms around you.
This is now.
Who needs forever?

We hurt.
We fly.
We burn.
And we die.
Will we return,
or become stars
to illuminate the way?

Until this world goes dark and cold,
it's your hand I want to hold.
When the jaws of the unknown open wide...

let's jump inside.

Cloudburst

joyful tears
alighting, burst;
dance on petals
in perfect step.

a Mother's love,
heart overflowing,
bathes the infants,
need is met.

ten thousand kisses
of adoration
fulfill the circle,
a promise kept.

vs.

News
Feed
Glutton.
Choose a side.
Choose completely.
Never relent.

Align!
Toe a line written in stone,
Archaic and unforgiving.
Fashion a noose on the hill.

Create what is right.
Debate, all that's left.
Truth survives at whose discretion?
Fable divides with no proof of lesson.

History is doomed to repeat... doomed to repeat... doomed...

The Hate in Our Bones

when the human experiment has long since failed,

when we've gone the way of Mesozoic beasts,

when advantages built with opposable thumbs

have succumbed to our belligerent hearts,

when science and religion have proven insufficient,

when Fibonacci, like God, has returned to form,

when we sink into legend like utopias lost,

will the host be permitted to heal?

will new life mutate and evolve?

will new cities rise from the ashes of ruin?

what will be unearthed and learned of our fate?

will they discover our inescapable flaw?

will they find the hate in our bones?

Risen from Dust

In this world, he can fly.
Here, magic survives.
Illusion is welcome.
Truth's hidden in the wings.

Beneath the proscenium and profusion of lights,
where dreams are encouraged, the child is embraced.
Danger is scripted, stripped of its power;
shadows genuflect, returned to their place.

Cast as hero, leader of the lost,
with a fairy to guide him and sword in hand,
he dispatches reality, floats like an angel,
never grows up, and will never ever land.

Apparition

From the day I first saw her,
the ending was writ.
She tempted my try
as she coddled my quit,

extolling my virtues
'til I grew obsessed,
so coveting the crown
she kept locked in her chest.

Infallible queen
I felt sure would be mine.
She built up my ego;
I knelt at her shrine.

She sang of salvation,
her voice so romantic.
She preyed on belief,
I was hopeful, pedantic.

She promised me more
than the best I could be,
and my eyes got so big
I could no longer see.

I bade her embrace me,
so desperate for proof.
Was it myth that I longed for
or tangible truth?

Each time I drew nigh
she would draw out her blade,
cut straight through my core
as my spirit decayed.

Still I followed my heart
down the road to perdition,
for loving perfection's
a fatal condition.

She led me through hell
to her final deceit,
where denied at the altar,
I died at her feet.

She dubbed me an error,
and I never would sit
on her throne fit for kings
who won't ever exist.

Fixed

my need

a crutch

your lips

a drug

the rush

then bliss

my fix

your love.

Sacred Ground

A visit to my past, this enchanted forest;
a childhood treasure, from simpler times,
fighting to survive, but alive and intact,
tucked in the belly of a town moving on.

Small speckled lizards jump, crawl, and skitter;
flash atop the ramparts, drenched in the sun.
Patrolling the entrance like tiny sentries;
gargoyles at the gates of a secret world.

The old stone slide provides thrilling passage,
worn smooth by innocents, the elements, time.
Alongside it, stairs, for more practical access,
or repeated climbs to unlimited rides.

At the bottom, the tall grass patiently waits;
bracing for old games, myriad new players.
Black rubber swings hang limp on their chains,
still catching their breath from perpetual flights.

Bowed bench tables, freshly painted grills,
prepare for the sound and the fury of feasts:
shouting, teasing, a riot of hands,
the unbridled laughter of insatiable youth.

On the edge of the wood, with mouths wide open,
lie trails for adventurers, daring the brave.
A gazebo stands vacant, to tempt the creative -
imaginations welcome, shared or alone.

The venerable trees look on with affection;
protecting my memories, safe in their shade.
A raft of ducks paddles the pond, in no hurry;
the young, behind mother, lined all in a row.

Psychic Pollution

Traffic's grown thick
on the road not taken,
ground to a halt
on the road that has been.

Every yellow wood,
all the black trodden leaves,
will soon be forsaken,
paved, with intention.
Our unslakable thirst
for relentless invention
breeds psychic pollution,
untenable dis-ease.

A Permanent Engagement

A permanent engagement.
Resigned declarations of codependence.
Hastily chosen allies,
turned foes in an unwinnable war.

Half-hearted attempts to kill.
Adequate strategies seldom present.
Psychological weapons
grow blunt from overuse.

Glancing blows pique interest.
Thrusts and parries keep a tenuous peace.
First aid fails in easing
the pain of deep malaise.

History predicts a stalemate.
Though a truce would seem the more bearable aim,
to injure and to suffer
make both sides feel alive.

Infantile

Like toddlers
pitching tantrums,
undone by emotion,
lacking apt language
or tactful expression.

I pound on the walls
while you sob in frustration;
we'll never fit squares
through the shape of a circle.

The End of Discussion

The latest fiction.
The exponential ME collective.
Where the well and the read tread lightly.
Where opinion seeps instantly from every page,
Unchecked, infecting like a plague.
Devouring the feed.
Risking nothing.
Proving nothing.

Pull up a chair. It's an I scream social.
Where they don't care to know you,
But they're damned pleased to media.
Where likes and shares are the sycophant's wares.
Cowards in masquerade troll for attention,
Parading their bias at every post,
To fan the flames of prejudice
And scorch the moral landscape.
Drunk on freedom, they laud thoughtless tongues.

All type. All bark. All hype.
Ignoble fools lay waste to a tool.
Thinking they will change the world,
When they can't even change their own minds.

Rectangled

towers of babble litter the sky.
satellites tumble and satellites spin.
more and more people make more and more toys.
and more human noise multiplies again.

we pixelate art beyond all decipher.
knowledge inferred, but obscured by the detail.
information surges, wisdom declines.
most of our days lived locked in our cells.

slaves now to access, virtually bound.
surface addicted, and numbing to depth.
the cyber sea rages, the current consumes.
we're rapidly sinking, caught up in the net.

interminable lines of communication
wind unabated around our necks.

Consider the Fish

What is the sound of suffering?
In man alone, such immense variation:
agony screamed with each fiber of being,
a harrowing groan through clenched teeth.

And from man's best friend comes a howl,
or sympathy begged with piteous whimpers.
A cat yowls when sick, or can curdle the blood
with an earsplitting screech, under siege.

Whether bawl or moan of the grizzly,
a scared bird shrieking with trembling beak,
the grunt or the squeal of a horse in distress,
no creature doubts pain that hears them.

But consider the cry of a fish.
Mute. Born missing this basic defense.
No plea for mercy. No summons for help.
Not a whisper in opposition.

Yet a man will torture these voiceless,
even gloat while they suffocate and writhe,
laugh as they're hanged alive from their faces,
to die on a lazy afternoon.

Imagine, however, this same man:
the roles reversed, betrayed by his nature,
submerged, alone, and frantic for breath,
with only death filling his lungs.

He too is silent, like a fish.

Verse 19

The wind stretches out
over empty streets,
caressing the trees,
making old music,
singing a forgotten song.

Bird and beast emerge
to explore the deserted world,
to restake their claim;
they move without fear.

The last winter moon ambles in,
setting the stage for the stars.
Orion's Belt dazzles
against a pitch-black sky;
celestial splendor now seldom seen.

Man looks on, as spectator,
behind windows,
over balconies,
across the water.
In need of answers.

Waiting...

2+2 is God?

Facts.
No? A veil?
Where origin stories clash,
there are axes to grind.
Where X crosses Y. Crucifixion.
Zero. Holy. Lines in the sand.

The agnostic treads lightly,
through ambiguous space,
on a tightrope between faith
in Numbers, or The Word.

Tethered to neither and
both demands balance.
More grounded? Perhaps.
Or much less sturdy?

A Zealot's Lament

I lost my voice,
singing her praises
at the top of my lungs.

I followed her lead,
and lost all sense of direction.

I questioned nothing,
sought no recompense,
and watched her leaving me,
from my knees.

Gift

The love you give,

like claws in my back,

tears me into ribbons

that I tie up in a bow.

Point of Departure

She awakens to birdsong,
a score for renewal,
whistles and warbles
that herald the dawn.
The morning cracks open;
she climbs out from cover.
Promise imbues her
with strength to move on.

Like the fledgling stretches,
gathering its courage,
she unfurls her wings
to initiate flight.

She leaves the nest,
with it, a foregone conclusion,
brave in ascent to unknowable heights.

Good Witch, Gypsy, Prophet, Sage

Lend me your pen,
that I may draw inspiration.
Grant me the fortitude
to set down my truth.
Suffuse me with ardor,
your immutable spirit.
Lead me through grief,
beyond pain, toward grace.

Teach me to laugh
in the face of the devil,
to sing and to dance,
when he strikes up his bow,
to walk in the light
until free of this body,
then open your arms up
and welcome me home.

The Feeling Begins

Eventide.
Multitudes adjourn.
Another day, like the rest, slowly dissolves.
The air is hot and dry, it weighs on tired shoulders.
The last shadows - those harbingers of the dark -
reach out along the ground, scale empty buildings.
Night promises everything.

We two, alive!!
Nascent minds awake.
Anticipation boils in our bellies.
Music fills our hearts to bursting,
sustains us, and obviates doubt.
The calendar spins.
Climb..

We move alone, with purpose. Unseen.
Winding between houses, ascending quiet streets.
We find our path up through the grass,
and soon overtake the rocks along the precipice.
Our breath begins to quicken. Our skin glistens with sweat.
Behind us, time is a fool;
it slows to a crawl, and dies in our wake.

Finally, we arrive at the peak,
a secret eden atop our surrogate city.
Sprawled out beneath us a vast grid is aglow, with
myriad intersecting channels and clustered columns of light.
We slowly make our way to the edge of the crest,
and sit down next to the moon.

In the distance, winged beasts flash across the sky,
soaring above the metropolis.
Further out, immense mountains stand in stunning
counterpoint to the dark, recumbent Pacific.
And where the earth surrenders to imagination,
we see only opportunity, in boundless supply.

The silence is euphoric,
and we do not speak.
But in a shared glance, it is understood:
Music, our passion, will bind us forever.
If we remain true, we cannot fail.

Then, from the absence, a primordial rumble.
Deep, sustained, bass notes arise,
cycling like a chorus of monks from an ancient world.
A transcendent melody cries out in yearning,
sonorous drums commence; beating of the trees.
Their hypnotic rhythm thunders through the hills,
and carries us into the future. Together.

All Through the House

my pen, on a bed
of crisp, blue-lined sheets,
lies dreaming of capable minds.

my screen, once aglow
like fresh driven snow,
drifts off, deprived of attention.

my keys feign sleep,
steal peeks at the ceiling,
and long for skillful caress.

my heart greets the dawn,
still savoring your kiss,
overwhelmed with inexpressible joy.

Sluggish

I'm on the ropes.
Nearly blind. Slits for eyes.
Head swinging like the pendulum
in my grandfather's clock.
Succumbing to trance.
Fighting to keep my knees from buckling,
I sway and stumble;
the lumbersome dance of the punch drunk.

Toe to toe with the Sandman.
Still undefeated, he's sure to fell me again.
As his final blow lands
I hear someone yell "timber!".
Grateful, I'm down for the count.

A Tragedy (In One Act)

Screams,
as he crashes through the door.
Without a knock. Without invitation.
The impact shakes every wall.
Family portraits hang untrue
in newly cracked frames,
frozen smiles belying disbelief.
Alarms wail for what is already lost.

He strangles time for two heartbeats.
His lifeless eyes, plotting, search the room,
do not abide any looking away.
The stench of him spreads out, crawling up stairs,
underneath beds, to torment sleep;
oozing through floors into the cellar,
to rot the foundation and leave permanent decay.

His destruction is swift. Complete.
In what seems only a breath, he is gone.
The neighbors gather, preparing their sympathies,
struggling to find reasons when there are none.

Those inside sit shocked and silent,
staring through tears at a turn in the road,
and begin the long wait for a fractured peace.

Heading for Home

A hush.
Chill October air.
New bags packed,
the worn left bare.
An empty home.

Every microphone,
speechless…
bowed in reverence.
Each seat, a mouth,
now soundly closed.
Both scoreboards,
forlorn, wait,
with none but the sun
and the moon to play;
familiar foes, a titanic struggle.

Old chalk lines dissolve
like specters into dust.
The last of the fowl fly south.
Regret, alone, will stay the winter,
and only promise warms the stove.

A Sure Thing

I am a tank,
treading a frozen lake.

You are a spark in the brush,
saddled to wind.

Time will not be kind.

A Willow Weeps

Spring brings joy
love abounds
two sow seed
in fertile ground

with special care
they tend the tree
love bears fruit
and two are three

nature thrives
through Summer blooms
but Fall comes fast
a tempest looms

violent storms
leave broken vows
near fell the tree
and cleave the bough

seasons change
at unknown cost
can fragile life
survive the frost?

Winter threatens
restless sleep
come Spring's return
A willow weeps.

White Flag (White Dress)

I loved the way you moved
(I loved who you might become)

I promised you the truth
(I promised not to care)

I hoped that you could bend
(I hoped that you would break)

I held you at a distance
(I held you to the light)

I exhausted your joy
(I exhausted your spirit)

I never lived up
(I never gave in)

I fell on my sword
(I finally smiled)

It seemed like the least we could do.

Anesthesia

savor your journey
through the altered states
a trip so expansive
replete with sensation
that you may find upon your return
you no longer feel anything at all.

For Julie

Near a congregation
of rocks by the shore,
you and I kneel,
as if joined in prayer.

We're hunting for stones
to skip on the water,
testing their merit
with nimble young hands,
delighted in finding
those flat and gone smooth,
stacking them into
fortuitous cairns.

Seraphic smiles
alight amidst laughter
arrived on the wings
of a merciful breeze.
It soothes for a moment,
our tender pink shoulders,
and gently lifts tresses
to tickle your cheek.

From a grill near the house
swirling gray puffs of smoke
rise up, as if spirits,
then sneak down the hill,
to tempt us with scents
of a plentiful feast;
our bellies and noses
both welcome the news.

Where trees kiss the lake
under weight of their leaves,
light paints the surface
like glass stained in gold.
While Grandpa's pontoon,
its mooring pulled taut,
glides on the wake
of a boat passing through.

But people, too, drift
as the years collect speed,
and I wonder if now,
you'd remember my voice.
A lifetime you've waited
for someplace called Heaven.
I wish I could tell you,
we've already been.

Bated Breath

Do not be too eager to arrive at conclusions,
crave endings, or final solutions.
For nothing quite thrills like riddle:
those exhilarating pages in the middle of a story,
an extraordinary vision, still hidden from view,
the power of a word not yet spoken to tease,
as it hovers on a lover's lips.

As magic's enchantment exists in the tricking,
but vanishes quickly with explanation,
a labyrinth's ends are oft frigid and dark,
while its heart fosters incandescence.

Epitaphs, after all, are etched in stone.
Photographs, captured moments
that long to be free.
Sometimes catastrophe
looms on the tongue.
Sometimes…
that word is "goodbye".

The Book Ends

We sit

Back to back

Between us

Worlds

Beginnings and endings

Romance and deceit

Climax and release

Comedy

Error

Yearning

Lament

Once upon a time

Time and time again

Over and over

Too much to remember

Enough.

Curfew

Twilight arrives
in muted violet.
"Ready or not!"
a child shouts.
Youth at play:
loud and fearless,
strong, dynamic,
poised to become.

Here inside,
where clocks
turn swiftly,
I sit on wheels
that rarely spin,
look only back,
losing faculties,
losing memories
to the ether.

As day retreats,
the moon creeps out
from under cloud,
a half closed eye.
Beyond the pane,
like lighted bugs,
faces flash
then disappear.

A hallowed voice,
grave but kind,
grown impatient,
calls me home.
I'm out of favors.
Dusk is falling.
And ready or not,
it's getting late.

Acquiescence

Does a blade of grass worry how tall it will grow?
Does a raindrop fear when and where it will fall?
Does a single star lose sleep reflecting on the dark?
Does a grain of sand trouble to battle the tide?

Lay down your suffering, my careworn friend.
You are the earth, the storm, the heavens, the sea.
Still your mind. Find strength in release.
Free your soul. Let go.

Acknowledgments

Love and very special thanks: Kim, for her expertise, and unwavering support - Mom, for her tireless help every step of the way, and her steady hand through the dark - Larry, for his vast wisdom and guidance - Rachel, my hero, without whom this book would have died a dream - my aquatic sons, past and present - friends and family, who offered kind words, and gave me the courage to stick with it - and the masters, who burst my heart open with this extraordinary art form. Finally, a bittersweet thank you to Covid-19, for reigniting my mind, and pausing the world.

About the Author

Christian Scott Green studied at the School for the Creative and Performing Arts and the Percussion Institute, and has spent his professional life composing and performing music on multiple instruments. His passion for rhythm, and deep love of the written word, converge in the world of poetry. He currently lives in Ohio; this is his first book.

Made in the USA
Monee, IL
13 June 2021